An Evaluation of Biological Inventory Data Collected at Tallgrass Prairie National Preserve
Vertebrate and Vascular Plant Inventories

Natural Resource Technical Report NPS/HTLN/NRTR—2009/247

Michael H. Williams
Kodge Data Services
150 Shady Branch
Benton, MO 63736

October 2009

U.S. Department of the Interior
National Park Service
Natural Resource Program Center
Fort Collins, Colorado

The National Park Service, Natural Resource Program Center publishes a range of reports that address natural resource topics of interest and applicability to a broad audience in the National Park Service and others in natural resource management, including scientists, conservation and environmental constituencies, and the public.

The Natural Resource Technical Report Series is used to disseminate results of scientific studies in the physical, biological, and social sciences for both the advancement of science and the achievement of the National Park Service mission. The series provides contributors with a forum for displaying comprehensive data that are often deleted from journals because of page limitations.

All manuscripts in the series receive the appropriate level of peer review to ensure that the information is scientifically credible, technically accurate, appropriately written for the intended audience, and designed and published in a professional manner. This report received informal peer review by subject-matter experts who were not directly involved in the collection, analysis, or reporting of the data.

Views, statements, findings, conclusions, recommendations, and data in this report are those of the author(s) and do not necessarily reflect views and policies of the National Park Service, U.S. Department of the Interior. Mention of trade names or commercial products does not constitute endorsement or recommendation for use by the National Park Service.

This report is available from http://science.nature.nps.gov/im/units/htln/ and the Natural Resource Publications Management website (http://www.nature.nps.gov/publications/NRPM/).

Please cite this publication as:

NPS XXXXXX, October 2009

Contents

Page

Tables iv

Abstract v

Acknowledgements vi

Introduction 1

Methods 2

    Expected Species Lists 2

    Compiling Existing Inventory Data 2

    The NPSpecies Database 3

    Inventories 4

    Inventory Certification 4

Results 5

Discussion 12

    Future Inventory Efforts 12

    Key Findings of Management Interest 13

Literature Cited 14

Appendix 1. NPSpecies bibliographic references for TAPR. 17

Appendix 2. NPSpecies Data Dictionary 19

Tables

page

Table 1. Count of species by park status categories at TAPR (NPSpecies 2009). 5

Table 2. Count of species by abundance categories at TAPR (NPSpecies 2009). 7

Table 3. Non-native plants, occurring on TAPR, with an Invasive Species Impact Rank (I-Rank) containing high..8

Table 4. Species on the park's local list which possess a state heritage program rank and/or other designated conservation status (State Heritage Conservation Rank/Status, Global, National, Subnational, and/or a Federal Status)... 10

Table 5. Number of species designated as present in park or probably present in HTLN parks (NPSpecies 2009).. 12

Abstract

The Inventory and Monitoring program of the NPS provides twelve basic inventories for park managers, including lists of species that occur in NPS units. Six hundred ninety eight species are certified on the list of vascular plants and vertebrates for Tallgrass Prairie National Preserve (TAPR). Based on a review of the evidence, 680 (97%) species were categorized as Present in Park, and 18 (3 %) as Probably Present. Fifteen species were Unconfirmed. In addition to documenting the presence of species, reviewers categorized the general abundance of 367 (53%) species and determined residency for all documented vertebrates with the exception of five (two mammals, two amphibians, one reptile). Species lists for TAPR can be queried from the Natural Resource Information Portal at http://nrinfo.nps.gov/Home.mvc.

Eighty one non-native species are documented to occur in the park. Of these are four fish, 17 birds, and 60 vascular plants. Non-native vascular plant species were assigned a NatureServe Invasive Species Impact Rank (I-Rank) based on impact to native species and natural biodiversity. Eleven of the 60 (18%) non-native plants found on TAPR received an overall I-Rank score that included the high category (i.e. most threatening).

A total of 10 species are considered to be of conservation status. One federally listed endangered species, Topeka shiner, is documented on TAPR. Two state threatened species (bald eagle, present in park, eastern spotted skunk, unconfirmed) are also listed. Future inventory efforts are discussed.

Acknowledgements

Thanks go to the inventory project researchers and their many volunteers including: Dan Fogell, Sue Fairbanks, and John Leonhart, University of Nebraska, Omaha, NE; Lynn Robbins, Missouri State University, Springfield, MO. Additional thanks go to NPS personnel including Park, Heartland Network, Midwest Region, and Washington Office staff. A special thanks to the staff of Tallgrass Prairie National Preserve for allowing access to the park during inventory and monitoring efforts.

Introduction

As part of the National Park Service's effort to "improve park management through greater reliance on scientific knowledge," a primary role of the Inventory and Monitoring (I&M) Program is to collect, organize, and make available natural resource data. A list of species known to occur in NPS units is considered a basic inventory need (see: http://science.nature.nps.gov/im/inventory/index.cfm). The I&M Program's Heartland Network (HTLN) recently completed inventories of vertebrate species and vascular plants at Tallgrass Prairie National Preserve (TAPR). In doing so, all existing data were cataloged, targeted field investigations were conducted, and species lists were certified by taxonomic experts. The primary goal of these efforts was to document at least 90% of the vertebrate and vascular plant species believed to occur in the park. This report provides a summary of results.

Methods

The HTLN followed a strategic plan of action set forth in an Inventory Study Plan (Boetsch et al. 2000) to complete inventories of vascular plants and vertebrate species. This plan was instigated by the Natural Resource Challenge in response to the National Parks Omnibus Management Act of 1998 and adheres to the requisite approaches delineated in Guidelines for Biological Inventories (NPS 1999) and the recommendations of the Service-wide I&M Program. The Inventory Study Plan identified steps to conduct a natural resource "information assessment" of existing park data. These steps included (1) developing master lists of species known or expected to occur in the park, (2) conducting field inventories, and (3) certifying the resultant species data.

> The term species (as opposed to organism) is generically used throughout this report to refer to unique taxa at the species level or below.

Expected Species Lists

In order to determine the completeness of inventory information, the HTLN developed lists of vascular plants and vertebrates expected to occur in the park. The master lists of birds were derived from the Kansas State University "Phenological Checklist of the Birds of Konza Prairie". The master list of fish was derived from county records supplied by Chris Mammoliti, Environmental Services Section, Kansas Department of Wildlife and Parks. Expected amphibians were derived from the U.S. amphibian distribution map internet site at http://home.bsu.edu/~00MJLANNOO/USamphibians.html. The range maps of Conant and Collins (1998) "A Field Guide to Reptiles and Amphibians of Eastern and Central North America" were used to derive expected reptile species lists. Any problems associated with synonymy were resolved by following Conant and Collins (1998). Jones et al. (1985) "Guide to the Mammals of the Plains States" was used to develop the mammal list. An initial compilation and evaluation of park floras was completed by Dr. Jim Bennett, National Wildlife Health Center, USGS BRD (Bennett 1995). Bennett compiled floras from "numerous sources: park lists, published journal articles and books, vegetation surveys, natural history reports, herbarium lists, park files and memoranda, and other miscellaneous park reports." Species names were standardized to USDA PLANTS (1999) and inconsistencies in infraspecific designations were resolved on a case-by-case basis.

Compiling Existing Inventory Data

Concurrent with development of expected species lists, HTLN staff worked with technical support from the Natural Resource Program Center (NRPC) to consolidate existing inventories. HTLN staff searched for existing inventory data, extracted species lists from the reports, labeled the lists with appropriate reference information, and forwarded the data to NRPC for processing.

HTLN staff mined inventory data from regional inventory databases, and transferred the network's Flora database. Staff also assembled bibliographic data concerning the primary park inventories. The Procite bibliographic database, NatureBib (aka NRBIB), was queried to produce an initial list of references. The lists were reviewed to ensure that each inventory: 1) included primary, rather than secondary, inventory data; 2) was based on observed, not expected, occurrences; and 3) was the result of professional surveys or research, rather than amateur observations. Park resource managers then reviewed and added to the lists.

HTLN staff searched for references to botanical collections as sources of species occurrence records. The process of searching regional herbaria for pertinent species records then commenced. The primary objectives were: 1) to find previously unknown collections; and 2) to document the current repository for older, known collections. The HTLN initiated a cooperative agreement with the National Wildlife Health Center (Biological Resources Division) to conduct computerized searches of regional and national museums and herbaria for park records of vertebrate and vascular plant occurrences. Given the limited timeframe, repositories with searchable collections databases were used. Dr. Jim Bennett, author of a summary of Midwestern NPS floras (Bennett 1995), was the principal investigator and was assisted with results of a search of the TAPR ANCS+ database collection provided by the HTLN.

> ANCS+ is a database management system developed by NPS to accession and catalog its museum collections.

The NPSpecies Database

NPSpecies is a master database for documenting the occurrence and status of all organisms in NPS units. The database includes standardized information associated with the occurrence of species, including scientific names and their synonyms (i.e. a local list or a standard list of species names), common names, abundance, residency, nativity, T&E status, and notes of particular management interest to a park. NPSpecies supports NPS staff and collaborators at the park, network, regional, and national levels by managing fundamental park-level species information, and making this information available to other applications and databases for more specialized analyses. A primary purpose for NPSpecies is to provide park managers, planners, and scientists with basic information on species occurrences and status for making decisions and working with other agencies, the scientific community, and the public for the long-term protection of park ecosystems (NPSpecies 2009).

Within NPSpecies, each species record is supported by evidence in the form of voucher specimens, references (scientific reports or datasets), and/or observation records that document the occurrence of the species in the park. Historical and currently-accepted scientific names from multiple taxonomic classification systems are cross-referenced using taxonomic standards (e.g., the Integrated Taxonomic Information System and the USDA PLANTS database) to allow for data integration and sharing across parks and with other agencies and organizations. In addition, parks are able to produce species lists based on the taxonomic authorities that are most accepted in their region and by their partner agencies.

Populating NPSpecies focused on three objectives: 1) transferring existing data; 2) including evidence for each record; and 3) verifying the accuracy of lists. As master species lists were compiled and transferred into NPSpecies a conservative approach was taken while assigning park status (e.g. present, probably present, etc.) to ensure that assessments of completeness were based on verifiable records. Many records imported from previous databases were unsubstantiated (i.e. not linked to a verifiable data source) and were classified as unconfirmed. Verification of vertebrate taxa was conducted by comparing digital records to original sources. The process proved valuable for assuring data quality as transcription errors, spelling mistakes, erroneous names, and synonymy problems were identified and corrected. In the process, park status (e.g. present in park, probable, unconfirmed) were also updated. After verifying and updating, any remaining species without evidence were assigned an 'unconfirmed' status.

Reliable status information is necessary to generate verifiable species lists for use in assessing inventory completeness. WASO I&M then completed the processing of these data and returned an NPSpecies database.

Inventories

Targeted field inventories were conducted to augment existing inventory data while addressing information gaps and high priority information needs. Two workshops were held during FY 2000 to assist in determining and prioritizing inventory needs (see appendix F in Boetsch et al. 2000). Regional taxa experts participated in these workshops and helped to revise project plans and priorities, and develop a greater awareness of taxa-specific inventory methods.

Subsequent to these initial steps, the HTLN began implementing inventories of amphibians and reptiles, birds, fish, mammals, and vascular plants. When completed, inventory reports were submitted to the HTLN and, once finalized, bibliographic data and the final report were uploaded to NatureBib. Species data (ie. taxonomic name, park status, abundance, etc.) and voucher data were uploaded to NPSpecies. Primary inventory data (ie. locations, events, etc.) and inventory specific data (i.e. bird counts, amphibian observations, etc.) were entered in a Microsoft (MS) Access database standardized to the current natural resource database template (NRDT) and uploaded to the NPS Data Store.

Inventory Certification

To support the objective of documenting 90% of vertebrate and vascular plant species expected to occur, subject matter experts (i.e. those involved with TAPR inventories) participated in the NPSpecies certification of taxonomic and attribute data for each taxa list. The process of certification is a data validation and quality assurance procedure for species checklists performed by subject matter experts most familiar with a particular taxonomic category. Taxon nomenclature are documented as well as park status, abundance, residency, and nativity.

Amphibian, reptile, and mammal certifications were compiled with current inventory data (Fogell 2003, Robbins 2005). Certification of the birds, fish, and vascular plants was conducted by HTLN staff. Generally, species lists were distributed as MS Excel worksheets and returned with revisions. Revised expected species lists containing a species park status (present, probably present, etc), abundance (common, uncommon, rare, etc), residency (breeder, resident, etc), and nativity as well as other attribute details were then updated (where necessary) via the desktop NPSpecies to reflect the current species' park status. These lists were then uploaded to the master online version of NPSpecies.

Results

Nineteen references (see Appendix 1) and 71 vouchers led to the certification of 698 species (NPSpecies 2009). In total, 680 species were categorized as Present in Park and 18 as Probably Present (Table 1). Additionally, 15 species were categorized as Unconfirmed. Unconfirmed species were ranked as such due to weak evidence supporting their existence on the park.

Currently 95% of the species on the park's species list are documented (i.e., categorized as Present in Park). If species listed as Present in Park and Probably Present are included in the calculation, the percentage of documented species rises to 98%.

Table 1. Count of species by park status categories at TAPR (NPSpecies 2009).

Park Status[1]	Bird	Fish	Mammal	Amphibian	Reptile	Vascular Plant	Total
Present in Park	136	29	28	8	23	456	680
Probably Present			14		4		18
Encroaching							
Unconfirmed	1		10	1	2	1	15
Historic							
Total	137	29	52	9	29	457	713

[1] Refer to the Appendix for definitions of Park Status categories.

Of the 680 species documented as present, reviewers assigned a general abundance category (e.g., common, rare, etc.) to 367 (53%) (Table 2). Reviewers believed additional information was needed before an abundance category could be assigned to the remaining 313 (47%) species. Results are available to NPS staff through the Natural Resource Information Portal at http://nrinfo.nps.gov/Home.mvc. The portal is the product of the Integration of Resource Management Applications (IRMA) project. To learn more see: http://www1.nrintra.nps.gov/im/datamgmt/docs/IRMA_ProjectBrief_v1.0.pdf.

Residency values (e.g., breeder, migrant, resident, etc.) were assigned for all documented vertebrates with the exception of five that were categorized as unknown. Unknown residency values were assigned primarily because it was unclear as to whether or not the species bred on the park. Non-natives documented to occur in the park (i.e., Present in Park) total 81. Of these are 17 birds, four fish, and 60 vascular plants.

NatureServe, in cooperation with The Nature Conservancy and NPS, developed a protocol to rank the impact of non-native invasive vascular plants (Morse et al. 2004). Through a series of standardized questions, non-native species are evaluated and assigned an Invasive Species Impact Rank (I-Rank) based on impact to native species and natural biodiversity. I-Ranks are categorized as high, medium, low, or insignificant. Eleven of the 60 (18%) non-native plants found on TAPR (NPSpecies 2009) received an overall I-Rank score that included the high category (Table 3). All are known to occur in the park (i.e., Present in Park).

A total of 10 species (Table 4) are listed by the Kansas Department of Wildlife and Parks and Kansas Biological Survey Natural Heritage Inventory as a species of conservation status. Additional NatureServe global, national, and subnational ranking status is provided. The 10 listed species included three birds, two fish, and five mammals. One federally listed endangered species, Topeka shiner (*Notropis topeka*), is documented on TAPR. Two state threatened species are: bald eagle (*Haliaeetus leucocephalus*) documented as present and the eastern spotted skunk (*Spilogale putorius*) listed as unconfirmed.

Table 2. Count of species by abundance categories at TAPR (NPSpecies 2009).

Abundance Category[1]	Bird	Fish	Mammal	Amphibian	Reptile	Vascular Plant	Total
Abundant		3	3			13	19
Common			12			50	62
Uncommon			11			137	148
Rare		1				137	138
Occasional							
Unknown	136	25	2	8	23	119	313
Total	136	29	28	8	23	456	680

[1] Refer to the Appendix for definitions of Park Status categories.

Table 3. Non-native plants, occurring on TAPR, with an Invasive Species Impact Rank (I-Rank) containing high.

Scientific Name	Common Name	Overall I-Rank	Ecological Impact[1]	Management Difficulty[2]	I-Rank Reasons Summary[3]
Alliaria petiolata	Garlic mustard	High / Medium	Medium / Low	Medium	Widespread, but commonly in highly disturbed systems. Although recent evidence points to garlic mustard starting to invade a greater range of geographic and ecological areas, including intact, healthy ecosystems.
Bromus inermis	Smooth brome	High / Medium	Medium	Medium	A threat to prairie and grasslands in the Midwest; alters rate of natural succession; changes native species composition; highly persistent.
Bromus tectorum	Cheatgrass	High	High	High / Medium	Found in all fifty states; widespread in abandoned fields, riparian vegetation, riparian meadows, grasslands, abandoned cropland, roadsides, and "waste places".
Carduus nutans	Nodding thistle	High / Low	Medium / Insignificant	High / Medium	Persistent in open areas, including prairies, grasslands, roadsides and areas of disturbance in dense woods; prolific seed production; seeds viable for up to 15 years.
Centaurea stoebe micranthos	Spotted starthistle	High / Medium	Medium	High / Low	In nearly every state in the U.S.; aggressive invader that easily invades disturbed areas then natural areas; common in open forests, prairies, barrens and other types of grasslands; increases erosion; out competes native species; moderately difficult to control.
Datura stramonium	Jimson weed	High / Low	Medium / Low	Unknown	Sometimes used as a hallucinogen, the species appears to be widespread throughout the U.S. in disturbed habitats and nearby natural areas. Little information is available regarding reproduction, dispersal, trends or ecological effects.
Holcus lanatus	Common velvet grass	High / Medium	High / Medium	High / Low	Widespread in the U.S. and present in every state (including AK and HI), except WY, SD, NE, MN, and FL. Apparently, it causes more negative impacts in the western U.S.

8

Table 3 (cont.). Non-native plants, occurring on TAPR, with an Invasive Species Impact Rank (I-Rank) containing high.

Scientific Name	Common Name	Overall I-Rank	Ecological Impact[1]	Management Difficulty[2]	I-Rank Reasons Summary[3]
Hypericum perforatum	Common St. John's wort	High / Medium	Medium / Low	Medium	Threatening natural areas in most areas of the U.S.; associated with a loss of biodiversity; forms dense monocultures; treatable if caught early, else, its prolific reproductive ability will prevent easy and inexpensive management.
Morus alba	White mulberry	High / Medium	Medium / Low	Medium / Low	Distributed throughout most of the U.S.; spread by birds and mammals; moderate capability of invading undisturbed areas.
Robinia pseudoacacia	Black locust	High / Medium	High / Medium	Medium	This is often a species of low-quality disturbed sites but it also invades some important, high-quality prairie and savanna ecosystems where it can significantly alter community structure and species composition.
Sorghum halepense	Johnson grass	High / Medium	Medium / Low	High / Medium	Severely inhibits pioneer grass species; massive size creates difficulties for the establishment of other plants; competitive edge over other species; one of the most frequently listed noxious weeds in the U.S.; control is difficult and costly.

[1] Subcategory of Overall I-Rank specifically addressing species negative impacts on native plant/animal populations/communities.
[2] Subcategory of Overall I-Rank specifically addressing difficulty of control.
[3] Summary reasons for NatureServe Overall I-Rank. For more information see the NatureServe Species Explorer at http://www.natureserve.org. These summaries reflective of NatureServe data last updated 6 February, 2009.

Table 4. Species on the park's local list which possess a state heritage program rank and/or other designated conservation status (State Heritage Conservation Rank/Status, Global, National, Subnational, and/or a Federal Status).

Bird	Scientific Name	Park Status[1]	State Heritage Program Rank/Status[2]	Federal Status[3]	Global / National / Subnational Status[4]	Global Short Term Trend[4]
Bald eagle	Haliaeetus leucocephalus	Present in Park	S1B,S4N / Threatened		G5 / N5B,N5N / S2B,S4N	Stable to increasing
Whip-poor-will	Caprimulgus vociferus	Present in Park	S3 / SINC*		G5 / N5B, NNRN / S3B	Survey wide decline
White eyed vireo	Vireo griseus	Present in Park	S2B		G5 / N5B,N5N / S2B	
Fish						
Spotted sucker	Minytrema melanops	Present in Park	S3 / SINC*		G5 / N5 / S3	
Topeka shiner	Notropis topeka	Present in Park	S2 / Threatened	Endangered	G3 / N3 / S2	Declining to stable
Mammal						
Eastern spotted skunk	Spilogale putorius	Unconfirmed	S1S2 / Threatened		G5 / N5 / S1	Large decline
Franklin's ground squirrel	Spermophilus franklinii	Unconfirmed	S2 / SINC*		G5 / N5 / S2	Declining to stable
Northern myotis	Myotis septentrionalis	Present in Park	S2		G4 / N4 / S2	Stable
Southern bog lemming	Synaptomys cooperi	Probably Present	S3? / SINC*		G5 / N5 / S3?	
Southern flying squirrel	Glaucomys volans	Unconfirmed	S3 / SINC*		G5 / N5 / S3	

*SINC=Species In Need of Conservation

[1] Refer to the Appendix for definitions of Park Status categories.

[2] The official species rank from the Kansas Biological Survey Natural Heritage Inventory (http://www.ksnhi.ku.edu/data/html/avail.htm) and endangerment status from the Kansas Department of Wildlife and Parks (http://www.kdwp.state.ks.us/news/Other-Services/Threatened-and-Endangered-Species).

[3] U.S. Endangered Species Act: Current status of the taxon as designated or proposed by the U.S. Fish and Wildlife Service (USFWS), and as reported in the U.S. Federal Register in accordance with the U.S. Endangered Species Act of 1973, as amended.

[4] The NatureServe conservation status, developed by NatureServe and its network of member (state) programs, of a species from a state/province perspective, characterizing the relative imperilment of the species. G = global (rounded), N = national, and S = subnational; 1 = critically imperiled, 2 = imperiled, 3 = vulnerable, 4 = apparently secure, 5 = secure; B=Breeding population, NR=Not rated. Refer to http://www.natureserve.org/explorer/ranking.htm#interpret for additional information on conservation status ranks.

Discussion

The NPS Inventory Strategic Plan states that "the ultimate goal is to establish an accurate inventory of all life forms within a park..." (NPS 2009, see also NPS 1992). The HTLN supports this goal by documenting over 80% of all vertebrates and vascular plants known to occur at TAPR. One result of these efforts is the compilation of reliable species lists. These lists, however sound, should always be considered incomplete. Inventory lists will change as new information about species distributions becomes available. The overall number of species designated as Present in Park or Probably Present is similar to similarly sized parks in the HTLN (Table 5).

Table 5. Number of species designated as present in park or probably present in HTLN parks (NPSpecies 2009).

Park	Bird	Fish	Mammal	Amphibian	Reptile	Vascular Plants	TOTALS	Park Size (ac.)
TAPR	136	29	42	8	27	456	698	10,894
HOME	81	31	41	6	9	304	472	160
HEHO	120	28	45	1	11	230	435	186
LIBO	224	-	38	13	13	332	620	200
GWCA	192	34	44	8	17	662	957	210
HOCU	274	15	40	21	25	457	832	280
PIPE	252	20	31	6	6	557	872	282
ARPO	111	65	33	17	40	332	598	389
EFMO	220	93	43	9	21	426	812	1,481
WICR	134	53	48	11	31	569	846	1,750
PERI	74	41	44	21	36	665	881	4,300
HOSP	114	52	49	22	45	910	1,192	5,549
CUVA	241	65	37	19	21	1,167	1,550	32,859
OZAR	167	122	55	29	45	880	1,298	82,196
BUFF	211	78	58	22	43	1,353	1,765	95,730

Future Inventory Efforts

While significant strides have been made in documenting the presence of vertebrate species and vascular plants, it is anticipated that additional survey efforts will be required to increase the number of documented species (i.e. Present in Park). For example, roughly half of the mammals are listed as probably present or unconfirmed and lack adequate documentation. Additionally, one state listed species is listed as unconfirmed. If species are thought to be Probably Present or Unconfirmed, follow-up surveys (perhaps targeted inventories?) are warranted or existing monitoring programs broadened to include searches for these species. Additional follow up inventories coupled with habitat studies may document their presence.

Reviewers assigned a general abundance category for all but 313 of the documented species (eight amphibians, 136 birds, 25 fish, two mammals, 23 reptiles, and 119 vascular plants). Reviewers also assigned a residency value for all but three. Continued monitoring of the species may provide for updated abundance and residency.

Based on the results of the data reported herein, future inventory recommendations include:

- additional resources to survey for species listed in Table 4,
- coupled with the above, focus on species listed as Probably Present, Unconfirmed, and Historic,

Key Findings of Management Interest

- The mammal inventory (Robbins 2005) noted that TAPR has a very good representation of available and historic habitat variables. However, observations of the Palmer Creek area indicate continued degradation of the riparian corridor including large deposits of droppings and the associated algae beds. Riparian vegetation and un-polluted surface water is essential for the species of mammals, including bats, that rely on continuous corridors of riparian vegetation for their movements, protection, and food.

- The amphibian and reptile inventory (Fogell 2003) found two species that are considered rare or in need of conservation in most states in which they occur: the massasauga (*Sistrurus catenatus*) and the Texas horned lizard (*Phrynosoma cornutum*). These were found in small numbers, but their existence on TAPR property affords the park great conservation value.

- The recent deer survey (Leonhart and Fairbanks 2004) noted that riparian habitat is limited on the preserve. While estimates of deer densities were low (for the preserve overall) impacts of deer use of riparian zones should be monitored for potential negative effects with changes in deer density.

Literature Cited

Bennett, J. P. 1995. Floristic summary of 22 Midwestern national parks. Wisconsin Cooperative Park Studies Unit, USGS, BRD.

Boetsch, J., M. DeBacker, P. Hughes, D. Peitz, L. Thomas, G. Wagner, and B. Witcher. 2000. A study plan to inventory vascular plants and vertebrates: Heartland Network. National Park Service.

Conant, R. and J. T. Collins. 1998. Reptiles and amphibians: eastern/central North America. Houghton Mifflin. Boston, Massachusetts.

Fogell, D. 2003. A herpetofaunal inventory of Tallgrass Prairie National Preserve, Homestead National Monument of America, and Pipestone National Monument within the Heartland Inventory and Monitoring Network. National Park Service.

Jones, J. K., Jr., D. M. Armstrong, and J. R. Choate. 1985. Guide to mammals of the plains states. University of Nebraska Press. Lincoln, Nebraska.

Kansas State University. No date. Phenological Checklist of the Birds of Konza Prairie. Maintained by the Konza Prairie LTER Program at http://www.konza.ksu.edu/.

Leonhart, J. and S. Fairbanks. 2004. Occurrence and relative abundance of white-tailed deer (*Odocoileus virginianus*) at Tallgrass Prairie National Preserve. Technical Report NPS/HTLN/TAPR/H6000A0100Z.

Morse, L. E., J. M. Randall, N. Benton, R. Hiebert, and S. Lu. 2004. An invasive species assessment protocol: Evaluating non-native plants for their impact on biodiversity. Version 1. NatureServe, Arlington, Virginia.

National Park Service. 1992. NPS-75: Natural resources inventory and monitoring guideline. National Park Service, Inventory and Monitoring Program.

National Park Service. 1999. Guidelines for biological inventories. Inventory and Monitoring Program, National Park Service. 10 pp.

National Park Service. 2009. Strategic plan for natural resource inventories, FY 2008 – FY 2012. Natural Resource Report NPS/NRPC/NRR—2009/094. National Park Service, Fort Collins, Colorado.

NPSpecies Proper: NPSpecies - The National Park Service biodiversity database. Secure online version. https://science1.nature.nps.gov/npspecies/web/main/start. Accessed May, 2009.

Robbins, L. 2005. Inventory of distribution, composition, and relative abundance of mammals, including bats, at Tallgrass Prairie National Preserve. Technical Report

NPS/HTLN/TAPR/ J6370040013.

USDA. 1999. The PLANTS database (http://plants.usda.gov/plants). National Plant Data Center, Baton Rouge, Louisiana.

Appendix 1. NPSpecies bibliographic references for TAPR.

1998. in R. Hiebert. Opportunities to enhance and maintain the tallgrass prairie ecosystem within the boundaries of Tallgrass Prairie National Preserve.

Barnard, I. 1999. Checklist of plants of Tallgrass Prairie National Preserve. Received as manuscript, including floristic list, in digital form from I. Barnard.

Fogell, D. 2004. A herpetofaunal inventory of Tallgrass Prairie National Preserve. Technical Report NPS/HTLN/TAPR/CA6000A0100.

Leonhart, J. and W. S. Fairbanks. 2004. Occurrence and relative abundance of white-tailed deer (Odocoileus virginianus) at Tallgrass Prairie National Preserve. Technical Report NPS/HTLN/TAPR/H6000A0100Z.

NPS HTLN. 2004. TAPR deer geodatabase. Dataset. ProductID: 1250 NPS MWR GIS Service Center.

NPS, Heartland Network. 2005. Tallgrass Prairie NPres mammal inventory geodatabase. Dataset.

NPS, Heartland Network. 2005. TAPR herpetofaunal geodatabase. Dataset ( ). ProductID: 1674 NPS MWR GIS Service Center.

NPS, Prairie Cluster LTEM. 1991. Special resource study: Z-Bar (Spring Hill) Ranch.

NPS, Tallgrass Prairie National Preserve. 1999. Tallgrass Prairie National Preserve: Resource Management Plan.

NPS, Tallgrass Prairie National Preserve. 2000. Final general management plan/environmental impact statement: Tallgrass Prairie National Preserve.

Peitz, D. G. 2003. 2003 fish community and Topeka shiner monitoring report. Annual report of activities conducted in 2003 under permits: U.S. Fish and Wildlife Service subpermit # SP01-07-01 under authority of permits PRT-704930 and PRT-697830 Kansas.

Peitz, D. G. 2003. Summary of baseline breeding bird inventories at Tallgrass Prairie National Preserve and Agate Fossil Beds National Monument.

Peitz, D. G. 2003. Summary of baseline breeding bird inventories at Tallgrass Prairie National Preserve.

Pietz, D. G. 2002. Fish community and Topeka shiner monitoring for Tallgrass Prairie National Preserve and Pipestone National Monument.

Pietz, D. G. 2002. Fish community and Topeka shiner monitoring for Tallgrass Prairie National

Preserve and Pipestone.

Powell, A. N. 2000. Grassland bird inventory for seven prairie park. United States Geological Survey. Wilson's Creek National Battlefield, Missouri.

Robbins, L. 2005. Inventory of distribution, composition, and relative abundance of mammals, including bats, at Tallgrass Prairie National Preserve. ( ).

Wanderning, W. O. 2002. An annotated checklist of vascular plants at Tallgrass Prairie National Preserve.

Wanderning, W. O. 2002. An annotated checklist of vascular plants at Tallgrass Prairie National Preserve. Unpublished report to the NPS.

Appendix 2. NPSpecies Data Dictionary

Park Status	The current status of each species in each park.	Applicable only to organisms with the *Local List* checkbox checked. The possible values reflect a combination of confidence, and availability and currency of verifiable evidence in NPSpecies.
Present in Park	Species' occurrence in park is documented and assumed to be extant.	Extremely high confidence that the species is currently in the park. A current, verifiable reference, voucher, or observation is included in NPSpecies.
Probably Present	Park is within species' range and contains appropriate habitat. Documented occurrences of the species in the adjoining region of the park give reason to suspect that it probably occurs within the park. The degree of probability may vary within this category, including species that range from common to rare.	Very high confidence that the organism is currently in the park. Verifiable evidence may exist in NPSpecies, but is not considered current enough to elevate the status to Present in Park. Efforts should be made to obtain current, verifiable evidence in NPSpecies to elevate the Park Status to "Present in Park". If reasonable efforts to obtain current, verifiable evidence are unsuccessful, then the Park Status should be changed to Unconfirmed, Historic, Encroaching, or False Report as applicable.
Unconfirmed	Included for the park based on weak ("unconfirmed record") or no evidence, giving minimal indication of the species' occurrence in the park.	Any confidence from very low to high that the organism is currently in the park. Verifiable evidence may exist in NPSpecies, but it is not considered sufficient enough to elevate the status to Probably Present, nor current enough to elevate the status to Present. Efforts should be made to obtain current, verifiable evidence in NPSpecies to elevate the Park Status to "Present in Park". If reasonable efforts to obtain current, verifiable evidence are unsuccessful, then the Park Status should be changed to Historic, Encroaching, or False Report as applicable.
Encroaching	The species is not documented in the park, but is documented as being adjacent to the park and has potential to occur in the park.	Extremely low confidence that the organism is currently in the park, but extremely high confidence that the organism is currently adjacent to the park. Verifiable evidence may exist in NPSpecies documenting the occurrence in the park, but it is not current. Potential invasive organisms are good candidates for this Park Status designation, either before they enter a park or after they have been eliminated from a park.
Historic	Species' historical occurrence in the park is documented, but recent investigations indicate that the species is now probably absent.	Extremely low confidence that the organism is currently in the park. Verifiable evidence exists in NPSpecies, but is not current. Extinct, extirpated or eliminated species are candidates for a Historic *Park Status* designation.
False Report	Species previously reported to occur within the park, but current evidence indicates that the report was based on a misidentification, a taxonomic concept no longer accepted, or some other similar problem of interpretation.	Extremely low confidence that the organism is currently in the park. Evidence exists in NPSpecies, but it cannot be sufficiently verified.

Appendix (cont.). NPSpecies Data Dictionary

Abundance	The current abundance of each organism in each park.	Applicable only to organisms with the *Local List* checkbox checked and a *Park Status* of "Present". The values attempt to balance abundance with suitable habitat, and temporal/behavioral considerations. In practice, the entered value should apply (although there are numerous exceptions) to the abundance in the most suitable habitat of the organism, and at the time that the organism is engaged in it's principle behavior in (e.g. breeding, migrating, hibernating, etc.), or most important behavior to, the park. A future generation of NPSpecies will address the coding of *Abundance* (and associated *Residency*) to separate out the temporal and behavioral aspects. The Data Source field for Abundance is available to provide a citation that specifically addresses abundance in more detail.
Abundant		**Animals:** May be seen daily, in suitable habitat and season, and counted in relatively large numbers. **Plants:** Large number of individuals; wide ecological amplitude or occurring in habitats covering a large portion of the park.
Common		**Animals:** May be seen daily, in suitable habitat and season, but not in large numbers. **Plants:** Large numbers of individuals predictably occurring in commonly encountered habitats but not those covering a large portion of the
Uncommon		**Animals:** Likely to be seen monthly in appropriate season/habitat. May be locally common. **Plants:** Few to moderate numbers of individuals; occurring either sporadically in commonly encountered habitats or in uncommon habitats.
Rare		**Animals:** Present, but usually seen only a few times each year. **Plants:** Few individuals usually restricted to small areas of rare habitat.
Occasional		**Animals:** Occurs in the park at least once every few years, but not necessarily every year. **Plants:** Not applicable.
Unknown		Abundance unknown.

Residency	Current residency classification for each ANIMAL species in each park.	Applicable only to ANIMALS with the *Local List* checkbox checked and a *Park Status* of "Present". The values attempt to balance temporal and behavioral considerations. In practice, the entered value should apply (although there are numerous exceptions) to the residency of the organism at the time that the organism is engaged in its principle behavior (e.g. breeding, migrating, hibernating, etc.) in, or most important behavior to, the park. A future generation of NPSpecies will address the coding of Residency (and associated Abundance) to separate out the temporal and behavior aspects. The Data Source field for Residency is available to provide a citation that specifically addresses Residency in more detail.
Breeder		Population reproduces in the park.
Resident		A significant population is maintained in the park for more than two months each year, but it is not known to breed there.
Migratory		Migratory species that occurs in park approximately two months or less each year and does not breed there.
Vagrant		Park is outside of the species' usual range.
Unknown		Residency status in park is unknown.

Appendix (cont.). NPSpecies Data Dictionary

Nativity	Nativity classification for each organism for each park	Applicable only to organisms with the *Local List* checkbox checked. If the park-status of an organism is not "Present in Park", then nativity represents the nativity if the organism were eventually confirmed in the park.
Native		Native The organism is native, or would be native, to the park (either endemic or indigenous).
Non-native		The organism is not native, or would not be native, to the park (neither endemic nor indigenous).
Unknown		Nativity status in the park is unknown.

The NPS has organized its parks with significant natural resources into 32 networks linked by geography and shared natural resource characteristics. The Heartland Network is composed of 15 National Park Service (NPS) units in eight Midwestern states. These parks contain a wide variety of natural and cultural resources including sites focused on commemorating civil war battlefields, Native American heritage, westward expansion, and our U.S. Presidents. The Network is charged with creating inventories of its species and natural features as well as monitoring trends and issues in order to make sound management decisions. Critical inventories help park managers understand the natural resources in their care while monitoring programs help them understand meaningful change in natural systems and to respond accordingly. The Heartland Network helps to link natural and cultural resources by protecting the habitat of our history.

The I&M program bridges the gap between science and management with a third of its efforts aimed at making information accessible. Each network of parks, such as Heartland, has its own multi-disciplinary team of scientists, support personnel, and seasonal field technicians whose system of online databases and reports make information and research results available to all. Greater efficiency is achieved through shared staff and funding as these core groups of professionals augment work done by individual park staff. Through this type of integration and partnership, network parks are able to accomplish more than a single park could on its own.

The mission of the Heartland Network is to collaboratively develop and conduct scientifically credible inventories and long-term monitoring of park "vital signs" and to distribute this information for use by park staff, partners, and the public, thus enhancing understanding which leads to sound decision making in the preservation of natural resources and cultural history held in trust by the National Park Service.

www.nature.nps.gov/im/units/htln/

Heartland Network

Natural Resource Monitoring

National Park Service
U.S. Department of the Interior

Natural Resource Program Center
1201 Oakridge Drive, Suite 150
Fort Collins, CO 80525

www.nature.nps.gov